LAUNCH

Welcome to *workplacelean*® – LAUNCH – bringing the power of **Lean** to your workplace. In LAUNCH you will learn the definition of **Lean**, understand the importance of **Value** from the customer's viewpoint, and identify the **Nine** types of deadly **Waste** within your workplace. You will **Map** your current process and apply **Lean** tools to improve your process. You will develop a **Future State**, identify targets for improvement and develop an **Action Register** for implementation of the improvements.

Training Objectives:

In this training session, you will learn:

➢ What is Lean?

➢ About the 9 common types of workplace waste

➢ To understand value added activities vs. non-value added activities

➢ To map your Current State and identify value and non-value added steps

➢ To understand and apply Lean principles and concepts

➢ To create conditions of an Ideal State for your process

➢ To map your Future State that resolves issues and eliminates waste

➢ To develop an Implementation/Action Register

The true power of *workplacelean*® is that it can be easily understood, used and implemented by employees at any level.

workplacelean®
% Des Moines Area Community College
DMACC Business Resources
1111 E. Army Post Road
Des Moines, IA 50315
1.800.362.2127 ext. 4919

www.workplacelean.org

Authors:

Bonnie Slykhuis
Collette Saylor
Gretchen Brink
Janet Drake
Emily Betz

LAUNCH

Table of Contents

Chapter 1

Focus on Lean

> **workplace*lean*®** *is a systematic* **approach to identifying and eliminating** *waste* **through continuous improvement by** *flowing* **the product or service at the** *pull* **of the customer.**

There are four words in this definition of **Lean** that are very significant.

1. **Systematic** means to approach the situation as a series of sequential steps. It starts with clearly defining a process which is a collection or series of individual tasks necessary to provide a service or produce a product. Then there is an analysis of each step to determine its purpose and value and then apply Lean tools to eliminate waste within the process. Rather than selecting problems at random and trying to fix them individually, we look at the whole process. This helps us to see how all of the process steps work together and identify opportunities for improvement.

2. **Waste** is defined as non-value added activity; steps that consume valuable resources of time, money, materials, and personnel without adding to the value of the product or service from the customers' viewpoint. Managers and employees need to be trained to identify and drive **waste** out of the system.

3. **Flowing** is the act of a product or service traveling uninterrupted through all the steps of a process until it reaches the customer. The goal of **workplacelean®** is that once a product or service enters a value-stream, it should never stop, or at least stop less frequently than before. **Flowing** a product or service focuses on a productivity goal. For **flow** to happen, employees must have the proper training, tools, processes and enough decision-making power to do their job.

4. **Pull** is producing or providing a product or service **at the demand** of the customer. We are accustomed to think of work as a type of funnel into which we toss people, materials, tools and procedures, and then put a lot of pressure on the top to **push** the product or service out. **Pull** is more about creating a pipeline with a faucet at the customer end. It is about creating a production system that

works smoothly so when the customer turns on the faucet we can quickly react to meet their demand. To **pull** a product or service through a system, we need to look at changing procedures and updating the tools and training of the employees.

Most organizations begin their Lean journey by having their employees attend a class like this. Then, by using Lean techniques and tools, they work to improve a **process**. As the teams experience success, and as more processes are improved using these Lean concepts and tools, fundamental changes occur – the organization and all the employees start to **THINK LEAN!**

A Brief History of Lean

Lean concepts were actually used long before the 20th century. Standardized and interchangeable parts facilitated the repairs on the battlefield by the French In the mid-18th century. Eli Whitney refined the concept and was able to build 10,000 muskets at an unheard of low price in the 1760's. Militaries everywhere began using continuous flow and standardized processes and fine tuning them through the 1800's. These ideas eventually made a slow transition into commercial manufacturing.

In 1910 through the 1920's Henry Ford used continuous flow and standardized processes, along with innovative machining practices to enable highly consistent assembly. He believed in Ben Franklin's advice that avoiding unnecessary costs can be more profitable than increasing sales. At the same time Frank and Lillian Gilbreth began to investigate the impact of human movement on the assembly processes. The *Process Motion Study* leads to the identifying of wastes in a process.

In World War II Consolidated Aircraft was able to build one B-24 bomber in one day. By implementing Lean principles and focusing on the human aspect of manufacturing Ford's Henry Sorensen was able to change that to one B-24 per hour within a two year period of time. Training within industry (TWI) was born to accommodate the training of women in this traditionally male workforce.

The end of the war saw Japan lead the acceleration of the development and implementation of lean methods. Taiichi Ohno at Toyota developed the elimination of waste and creation of value concept. Employees were valued and given increasing amounts of authority and control on the shop floor.

W. Edwards Deming went to Japan in the early 1950's to give a series of lectures on statistical quality control, demonstrating that improving quality can reduce cost. Toyota embraced these concepts and implanted into the Toyota Production System (TPS). Ohno and Sheigeo Shingo continued to refine and improve TPS with the development of pull systems, Kanban and quick changeover methods.

In the 1970's the term "Lean" was first coined by John Krafcik in his MIT master thesis on Toyota. James Womack and Daniel Jones books *The Machine That Changed the World* and *Lean Thinking* with Daniel Roos popularized the term.

The primary characteristics of **Lean** are;

- Specify value from the perspective of the customer
- Define the value stream for a product, then analyze the steps in the process to determine which are waste and which are value-added.
- Continuous flow
- Create pull between process steps – made to order in the exact amount required
- Move toward continuous improvement – in quality and eliminating waste.

By 2000 lean methods were beginning to move from manufacturing to the office, healthcare, education, governments and other administrative environments.

Lean is about **creating value**, *not just eliminating waste*, and **empowering people**.

*The above information was compiled from the following sources.
"A Brief History of Lean" – Lean Enterprise Institute
"A Brief History of Lean" – Strategos – Consultants, Engineers, Strategists

Lean IS about

- **improving organizational and employee productivity.** Lean helps people to better understand their work processes and the reasons for each step.

- **reducing and/or eliminating costly wastes and reducing errors.** Employees who do the work often have ideas about how to fix problems or change work to make it better, faster, easier and more cost effective.

- **involving and training all employees in improving work processes.** Training employees to use tools of Lean will help your organization reach its Lean goals more quickly.

Working smarter - not harder!

Lean IS NOT

- **a method to reduce the organization's headcount.** If an organization uses Lean as a cover for reducing staff, workers will stop contributing to process improvement efforts and Lean will fail.

- **an abdication of managerial authority or responsibility.** Managers must believe they have a role in process improvement and not block efforts or fail to encourage their employees to participate. In fact, if used appropriately Lean can make a manager's job much easier. It teaches employees to identify and evaluate problems and propose possible solutions. It allows more time for managers to be proactive rather than reactive.

- **a one-shot quick fix for problems.** Lean is an ongoing process. It must be continuous to address ongoing changes in customers, technology, people and markets. Processes have to continuously change and improve for an organization to remain competitive.

Most importantly, **Lean *is not* about finding fault in people.** Bad processes make it easy to blame people, even when they are doing the best they can with limited resources and knowledge of the process. To avoid this, Lean looks at how we can change the process to ensure people are working most effectively. **Lean *is* about finding and reducing wastes in processes.**

Benefits of Lean

- **Standardized work**
- **Identification of training needs**
- **Error-proofing**
- **Understanding of processes**
- **Reduced work steps**
- **Staff efficiency**
- **Improved communications**
- **Electronic & automated systems**
- **Improved service**

Successful Lean Organizations

Organizations that are successful in leaning their operations build a culture that supports and fosters these foundations of workplacelean®:

- **High employee engagement:** Knowing that every employee has valuable information to share and ideas for improvement. Having methods to cultivate the information/ideas and empower employees to make decisions within their parameters.

- **Respect for the individual:** Believing in and trusting employees to do what's best. Treating them with respect and continually showing that you value their contributions.

- **Flexibility to adapt to change:** Removing waste and roadblocks from processes that allow people in work areas to be proactive rather than reactive. Having efficient and timely methods for evaluating performance and reacting to changes.

- **Continuous improvement of work processes:** Having methods or systems to regularly evaluate work processes for improvement opportunities.

- **Organization-wide implementation:** Having consistent and meaningful expectations for quality improvement throughout the organization. Often driven by strategic initiatives and incorporated into employee job performance expectations.

Chapter 2

Determining Value in Your Process

> A **Process** is a collection or series of individual tasks necessary to provide a service or produce a product

If you were to observe and document someone making coffee here are steps you might see.

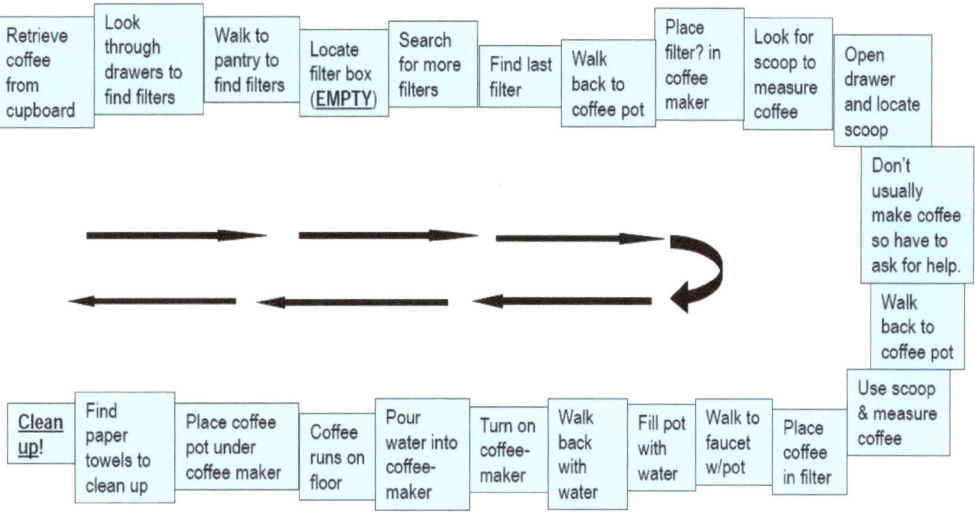

Every process contains steps or activities that contribute to the end product and some that simply waste time, energy, personnel or resources. The next step in process improvement is to identify Value Added and Non-Value Added activities.

Identifying Value

Value can be defined in terms of what is valuable to your **customer**. It need not be monetary or commercial. It is an action that adds value directly to the product or service that they want. It is important not to assume the wants and needs of your customer; find out! Just because a process step has value to you, doesn't mean that it is of value to the customer or the next step in the process.

Everything done by an organization can be evaluated by one criterion: value. It is not the value we put on the process, product or task. It is much simpler than that...What is the customer willing to pay for to produce this product or service?

- **Value Added Activity** is an action that adds value directly to the product or service. We often say it changes the form, fit or function of the product or service. Examples are entering customer orders, assembling parts, checking quality, communicating status and purchasing materials.

- **Non-Value Added Activity** is an action that adds no value from the customer's viewpoint.   Reworking defects, excessive product inspections, redundant signatures, multiple file copies, multiple stacking, staging or repositioning of parts.   These activities add nothing to the value of a product or service, but consume valuable resources, such as time, materials and personnel.

  - **Essential = Required.** These are non-value added activities that we have no control over and cannot remove from the system.   They often include government regulatory steps, accounting procedures and other activities that must be performed that the customer really would not choose to fund but has no choice.

  - **Pure *Waste.*** We are looking for the non-value added activities that are pure waste that the customer would never pay for if asked. Examples would include re-entering data into multiple systems; making safety copies of forms; repeated moving of parts; materials or information; and fixing errors and defects. *See the 9 types of Deadly wastes in Chapter 3.*

In this example the Non-Value Added Activities have been shaded a different color.

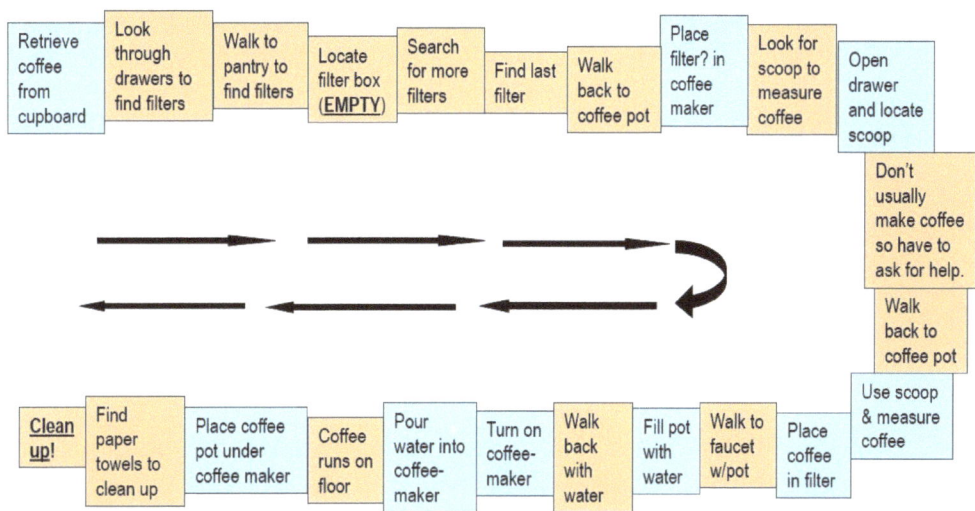

> **The lead time for a product or service typically consist of 95 to 97% Non-Value Added Activity before Lean is applied.**

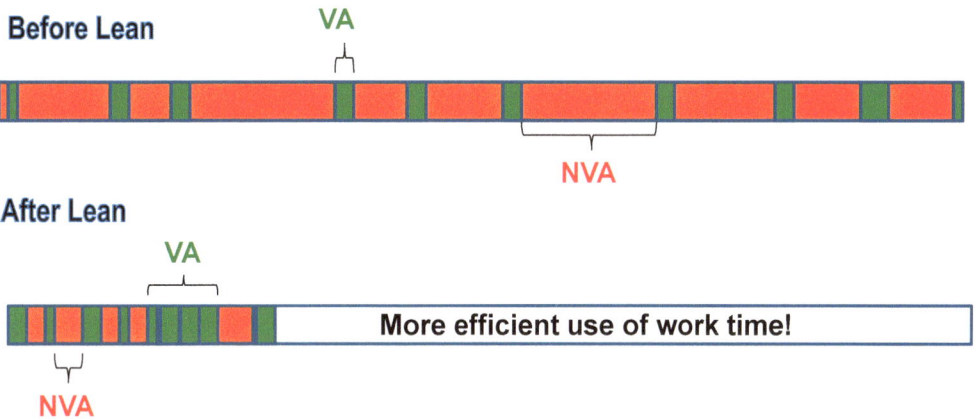

Can you think of something that occurs in one of your work processes that adds no value to your product or service?

Chapter 3

Understanding Wastes

Waste (Non-Value Added Activities)

Wouldn't it be nice to finish the day with your paperwork caught up and all of your workspaces organized? Have all tasks completed because you received clear, correct and accessible information? Your co-workers and other departments would be collaborating all resulting in happy customers. **Waste** needs to be recognized and eliminated before you can anticipate these happy results.

Here are some symptoms that waste and process problems exist: Duplication of effort; road blocks; too much walking; missed deadlines; overtime; worker fatigue. The list seems endless. How many do you see in your daily work?

Your work is made up of all kinds of processes. Within every process there is **Waste.** Waste can be defined as any activity that is not adding value to your product or service. It is a **waste** of valuable resources: time, money, materials and/or personnel. These efforts also add no value to your product or service from the **customer's viewpoint**. They are not willing to pay for it.

To eliminate waste, you must first be able to identify it. Lean experts have identified nine common forms of waste that exist in all work environments which negatively impact efficiency and productivity.

Nine types of Deadly Waste

- Defects/Errors
- Overproduction
- Waiting
- Unnecessary Transport
- Over-Processing
- Excess Inventory
- Excess Motion
- Underutilized People
- Confusion

Begin identifying wastes in your work. The first step in improving processes is to recognize the wastes. As we define each type of waste, write down examples of that waste that you see in your current work environment.

Defects/Errors
Something is missing or incorrect

- No standard procedures
- Wrong information/parts
- Missing information/parts
- Defective parts
- Poor form design

Waste from defects/errors occurs anytime the product or service is not done right the **first time**; sub-standard product or information is received from a previous step. This requires you to do rework or take extra steps to correct the error. Often defects/errors can be caused by limited systems capabilities, people not understanding what is required, lack of system maintenance, or poor handling of information/parts. Defects and errors slow down the process, make it unreliable and affect customer satisfaction.

What **defects/errors** do you see in your process now?

_____

_____

Overproduction
Producing sooner or more than is needed

- Producing it "Just in case we need it"
- Unsure of what is needed or how much
- Collecting more information/parts than are needed
- Creating reports that are no longer needed
- Producing more than the customer orders

Waste occurs when people overproduce because they are unsure of exactly what is required. Sometimes employees overproduce as a possible cover for faults in the system or to stay busy. Examples would be making and filing extra copies because forms might get lost or making product that exceeds customer demand.

What activities do you see in your process that are not needed or result in **overproduction**?

_____

_____

Waiting

Downtime when people, information, equipment or materials are missing or not available

- Waiting in a queue or waiting for next batch to arrive
- System/equipment down
- Waiting for approvals
- Waiting for information from customers (internal/external)
- Working around information gatekeepers (those unwilling to share information)
- Unreliable or inconsistent delivery systems

Waste occurs from waiting when a product or service slows or stops because information, approvals or parts have not been received when needed to continue the process flow. Waiting can be increased if people are unclear of expectations, unaware of next steps, unsure of where or how to find needed information, or have poor delivery systems.

What do you constantly have to **wait** on to complete your work?

_____

_____

Unnecessary Transport

Moving or transporting anything that does not lead to value-added activities

- Information/parts hand-offs
- Circulating paperwork for signatures
- Report distribution
- Paper routing vs. electronic routing
- Placing processes or functions based on space vs. workflow
- Copy machine/fax/mail runs

When organizations grow and available space decreases, there is a tendency to put things where they fit rather than where they best align with work processes. This increases the movement of people and things. In addition, organizations that rely heavily on the manual movement and passing of information/parts also increases the transportation

What information or items do you see **transported unnecessarily**?

_____

_____

Over-Processing

Any effort or additional process steps that do not add value to the product or service from the customer's view

- Redundant data entry
- Extra copies
- Providing more information/parts/materials than is needed
- Collecting and/or handling extra information/parts
- Multiple checks of information/parts
- Following "old practices" vs. "best practices"

Waste from over-processing happens when unnecessary information/ materials is collected or extra steps are taken that are not essential. Organizations that fail to periodically re-evaluate their steps and methods are more likely to over-process. Additionally, organizations who do not or are not equipped to share data across departments or locations suffer from over-processing.

What examples of **over-processing** have you seen in your process?

_____

_____

Excess Inventory

Inventory levels of parts, supplies, forms, etc., in excess of what is needed in a reasonable period of time

- Surplus forms, computers, materials
- Outdated items
- "Safety stock"
- Non-functioning items
- Retaining documents longer than required
- Safety files to "CYB" (Cover Your Behind)
- Inventory in excess of customer demand/need

Waste from excess inventory occurs when a supply of information or product is created beyond what is needed or can be used within a reasonable period of time. Excess Inventory can also be caused by failing to dispose of items or information once it is no longer of value.

What in your workspace is outdated or in **excess** of what's needed to perform your job?

_____

_____

Excess Motion

Any movement of people, machines or equipment that does not add value to a product or service

- Looking for… anything!
- Motion related to poor workspace organization
- Multiple computer screens or filing systems
- Paper lists vs. electronically shared updated lists
- Inadequate tools for the task

Waste from excess motion is any activity or step that exceeds what is optimal for doing your job in the most efficient way possible. When an item or information is not where you need it, when you need it or how you need it, excess motion is required to retrieve it and continue the process.

What **extra steps or motions** do you take to complete your tasks?

_____

_____

Underutilized People

People's skills and abilities are not used to their full potential

- Limited authority and responsibility for basic tasks
- People not empowered and encouraged to solve problems
- Lack of training in critical skills or job functions
- Little collaboration across departments
- Existing employee skills not recognized

Organizations that do not empower their workforce to make basic decisions about their work or that fail to provide adequate tools, development and training for employees to do their job waste time and energy and underutilize their people. This also occurs when managers or supervisors want to control all employee activity.

What examples have you seen of **people not being utilized** to their full potential?

_____

_____

Confusion
People are unclear about tasks and/or how to perform them

- Absence of standards (written and visual)
- Lack of training
- Limited understanding about the process
- Unclear requests for work
- Unaware of resources or contact people to help perform work

Waste from confusion occurs every time you have to stop and think about what happens next, redirect your thoughts, or re-evaluate where something is in the process. Lack of standardized procedures and unclear requests for work are primary causes of confusion. Confusion on the job increases defects/errors, creates excess motion and increases the level of negative "social" effects employees' experience.

What confusion exists in your job for you or others?

_____

_____

Waste takes a toll on each of us every day resulting in physical and emotional fatigue, increased stress, frustration and low self-worth. This can result in lack of trust and indecisiveness. In an environment filled with waste, it is difficult to be productive and a great deal of effort is expended for minimal results.

The goal of Lean is to:
1. Eliminate **Waste** in work processes
2. Flow **Value** to the customer

Small Group Activity:

Identifying Wastes

Working in 2-3 person teams, identify three examples of waste within **your current work process.**   Be ready to share your examples with the rest of the group and tell why your team picked these wastes.

Wastes:

Chapter 4

The Basics of Process Mapping

> **A process map is a visual representation of the steps performed to provide a service or produce a product.**

Process mapping helps you

- Identify all steps of the process
- Evaluate which steps are Value Added and which are Non-Value Added
- Gain a deeper understanding of the entire process
- Identify opportunities for improvement
- Create standards
- Build consensus and ownership for improvements

It's about the process - NOT the people.

Let's begin by defining the scope of your project. What is to be accomplished by analyzing your process?

Defining the Project Scope

The Project Scope helps determine the parameters of your mapping project. It should be shared with participants prior to your mapping sessions to ensure everyone understands what you will be working on and working towards. The list below is example of what a Project Scope document should include.

1. Name or description of the process being reviewed
2. Reason for the evaluation
3. Beginning and End steps of the process to be mapped
4. Names of participants. The process stakeholders (those having responsibility for steps in the process), customers and functions supporting the process such as IT, supervisor and upper

management need to be involved. It's also beneficial to have someone who has nothing to do with the process be involved to challenge the group.

5. Project champion or person responsible for ensuring the project stays on task and is completed

6. Goals or desired outcomes you want to achieve as a result of mapping and evaluating the process

7. Metric goals or targets. How the project will be measured to determine level of success. Baseline data for the metrics identified should be assigned to someone for collection prior to the mapping sessions.

8. Training dates, timelines and checkpoints

Why Map the Current State

Often within work areas or departments, functional groups do not fully understand the tasks other groups perform in the process flow. By mapping out the **Current State** in detail, the entire team sees the roles and responsibilities of other members allowing them to more fully understand the entire process. This experience is priceless in breaking down the barriers between functions as the team works together to create an efficient flow across all departments involved to best serve all customers.

There are many benefits of using process maps, because people have limited understanding of an organization's processes and usually visualize them differently; a process map can build understanding and often create the 'aha' moment necessary to drive action, improvement or change. Visual representations of how we do things helps to create understanding of where we are and sometimes how we got here. You can't set a new course or plan a new route if you don't know where you are to begin with.

Current State maps are one of the foundations of continuous improvement. You have to fully understand where you are in order to make improvements. This full understanding doesn't come from discussing a process in a conference room. Everyone involved must be able to see how the process as it currently exists before discussing ways to improve it. There is no substitute for actually seeing how things are done now.

Mapping Guidelines

- Map as if creating a training document. This means including small steps that are typically taken for granted such as printing, stapling, counting, staging, reviewing, etc.

- Map chronologically as a timeline.

- Use an 80/20 rule - Does this process step happen most (80%) of the time or is it an exception? Concentrate on identifying the process steps that take place the majority of the time.

- Use positions rather than names of people.

- All steps must lead to the next step or have an 'end of process' symbol.

Process Map Components

- **Process Steps** are the tasks that are performed to flow the process to provide the service or produce the product. Write steps vertically on 3x5" yellow Post-it® notes.

- **Decision points** are junctures in the process where activities can flow in two directions. Decisions are phrased as questions that are answered as either yes or no, written on blue 3x3" Post-it® notes.

- **Issues** are problems that exist in the process that cause the process to slow down, stop or require backtracking, written on green 3x3" Post-it® notes and collected and placed either on the map or the Issues flipchart.

- **Potential Solutions** are the "proposed" remedies to issues and inefficiencies identified by the team. These proposed solutions are not necessarily the final solutions the team will recommend to implement improvements. These are written on pink 3x3" Post-it® notes and collected and placed either on the map or the Potential Solutions flipchart.

- **Swim Lanes** identify different departments or key stakeholders in the process. These are much like lanes in a swimming pool in that everything that occurs in that lane is the responsibility of that stakeholder. In the example below the Hiring Supervisor is responsible for all the steps in their lane.

- **Handoffs** are indicated by arrows crossing into or over another stakeholder's swim lane. This is where work is "handed off" to another department or person. Note: Arrows are not needed between each step within the same swim lane.

- **Rework** happens anytime you need to take extra steps because information or parts are not correct or compliant with what is needed.

In the electronic map example we indicate rework by red arrows. When building a map with Post-it® notes you may or may not have red arrows available.

- **Other mapping symbols**

  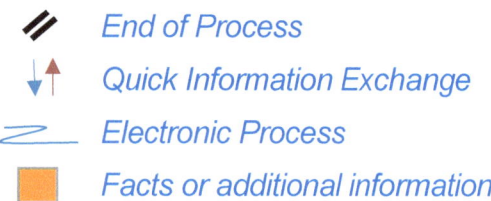

  End of Process

  Quick Information Exchange

  Electronic Process

  Facts or additional information

Below is are examples of the electronic version of partial process maps. Once mapped by hand on a wall of paper, the map can be captured in Excel or mapping software such as Microsoft® *Visio* for sharing with others or to use as training documents.

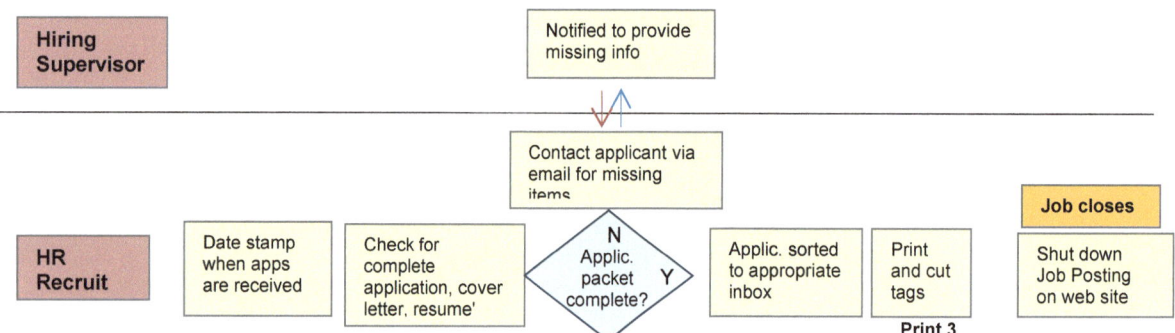

Additional map information can be easily added to the map based on the needs of the group. In the example above, the group wanted to know how many items were printed. You can also track other manual steps such as signatures and copying. Below they chose to include processing time for steps and metrics for the entire Current State map.

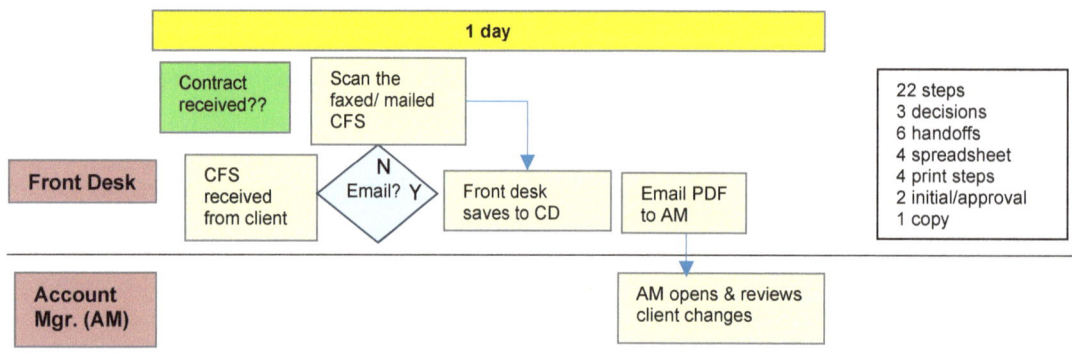

In the next example, additional information was included using the orange box to clarify a step and a green issue was added noting a problem that occurs at this point.

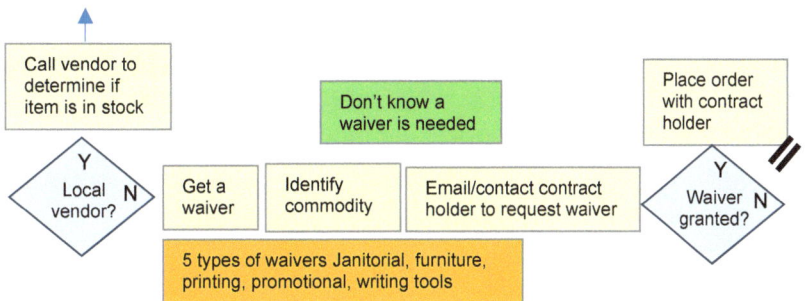

Roles in Mapping

Map Facilitator

- Leads the group involved in mapping
- Places steps on the map
- Asks clarifying questions
- Keeps group moving forward

Process step writers

- Target of 8 words or less
- Extra information should be written an orange Post-it® and placed near the process step it is referencing (i.e. form or screen information, names or details)

Decision point writer

- Decisions -- short yes/no questions

Group Roles

- Help each other capture all issues and potential solutions on the map or on a separate flip chart
- Stay engaged in the process mapping activity…avoid side conversations
- Respect the "One Person at a Time Speaking" Rule
- Respectfully challenge each other on process steps to ensure accuracy and understand value
- Focus on the process steps, not on people – use position name rather than persons names
- **Map as it is now – not how "it should be"**

Map the Current State

Analyze the Current State

Team Activity:

Identifying Value/Non-Value Added Steps

As a Team, review each process step and determine which category (below) that step falls into and mark that step with the corresponding colored dot. This activity helps to visually show you where the greatest opportunities for improvement exist. During creation of the **Future State** Map these dots will help prompt improvement discussions.

○ **Value Added Activity = *No color*.** Identify actions that add value directly to the product or service as determined by the customer. *Example:* depositing funds, entering correct customer information into information system, assembling parts.

● **Value added activity needing improvement.** Identify process steps that are valued added but could be improved. *Example:* converting a paper form to an electronic form with automatic workflows and electronic approvals, reorganizing work area so parts/products flow from one step to the next without being routed or staged in between.

○/● **Non-Value Added Essential = Required.** These are non-value added activities that we have no control over and cannot be removed from the system due to government, organization or certifying requirements. The group must determine if these steps can be improved upon (green) or must remain as is (no color). *Example:* Oversight documents, procedures (HIPPA, EEOC, FERPA) and other activities that must be performed that the customer would not choose to fund, but has no choice.

● **Pure Waste.** Identify non-value added activities that are pure waste that the customer would never pay for if asked. *Example:* making paper copies of forms that are never referenced, rework steps, routing or staging steps.

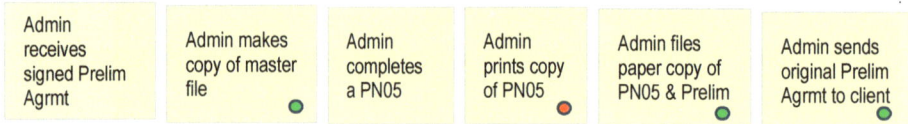

Questions that may help you determine if an activity is value added or non-value added:

1. Is the step value-added or supports a value-added step?

2. Is there a better way to do the step?

3. Would the customer be willing to pay for this step?

Team Activity:

Categorizing Issues

Teams should categorize the issues and potential solutions into general broad categories. This will allow us to identify trends and problem areas that need to be addressed in the future state map and the action register. Examples of categories might include: *training, equipment, work scheduling, IT programming.*

Chapter 5

Application of Lean Tools

Now that you have mapped your **Current State** process and identified the wastes and activities needing improvement we can now apply **Lean Tools** to remove the wastes.

Depending upon the situations that are represented on the **Current State**, some tools will have a bigger impact than others. However, it is a mistake to overlook ANY tool when focusing on driving waste out of a system.

Lean Tools

✓ **Standardized Work**

✓ **Error-Proofing**

✓ **Visual Controls**

✓ **Work Area Layout**

✓ **Workspace Organization - 5S**

✓ **Batch Reduction**

✓ **Cross-Training**

✓ **Work Balancing**

Standardized Work
Use of consistent work methods for improved results

An important and relevant Lean concept to any work activity is Standardized Work. If work is standardized in a process, the variation in the outcomes is reduced significantly and the output is more predictable, reliable and repeatable.

Standardized work means consistency comes before quality. To be able to drive waste out of a system, we must have a standardized series of tasks. A consistent system with poor quality can be improved; however, a chaotic system with poor quality cannot.

- **Standardize work steps**
- **Best, easiest way to do a task**
- **Facilitates performance measurements**
- **Identifies and eliminates sources of errors faster/easier**
- **Basis for effective new employee training**

Make it easier for people to do it the right way!

Identify processes in your workplace which are not standardized and list them below.

_____

_____

_____

_____

_____

_____

_____

_____

_____

_____

Error-Proofing
Using tools to detect and prevent errors which improves quality

The main purpose of Error-Proofing is to prevent errors from happening, rather than detecting errors later. The goal is to find the source of the error and fix it.

- **Colored files/binders/paper**
- **Checklists**
- **Templates**
- **Log sheets**
- **Screen prompts**
- **Forms**

> **It is estimated when an error is passed on to another area, the cost of the error becomes ten times the initial cost. The next pass is conservatively estimated to be 100 times the initial cost. Your goal should be to eliminate any type of rework!**

Are error proofing tools used in your workplace? List them below.

_____

_____

_____

_____

_____

_____

_____

_____

_____

Visual Controls
Unmistakable visual cues which make standards and activities obvious and maintain order

Visual Controls are simple visual cues that everyone can understand quickly and with very little thought. Visuals can be used to provide feedback on performance levels, give directions, define the location and order of items, and provide warnings. The Department of Transportation does a good job of providing visual controls with road lines, signs, labels, and color-coding.

- **"How we are doing" at a glance**
  - **What we are working on**
  - **The level of performance**
- **Provides information immediately to people in the area**
- **Promotes communication**
- **Visible management metrics**

Visual Controls must be simple and up-to-date to be effective.

Below list possible places to utilize visual controls in your work area.

_____

_____

_____

_____

_____

_____

_____

_____

_____

_____

_____

Work Area Layout
Improved productivity through physical location of work stations, task organization and work flow management

The design of the workspace or Work Area Layout should be built upon the flow of the process from one person to another. Quite often in organizations, the layout of the workplace evolves over time as employees are added and as facilities are available without any consideration of process efficiency. People are put where they fit, rather than where they belong to make the process work effectively and improve the flow. Well planned work area layouts facilitate cross-training.

- **Build layout with the flow of the process and people in mind**
- **Arrange computers/equipment to match the processing sequence**
- **Try to use smaller machines**

Below list any ideas you have to improve your work area layout.

_____

_____

_____

_____

_____

_____

_____

_____

_____

_____

_____

_____

Workspace Organization (5S)

Organization of the workspace for improved efficiency

Organization of workspace is often referred to as 5S and is based upon a place for everything and everything in its place. Clutter, outdated supplies, old equipment, dirty workspaces, excessive inventory all have the potential to slow down the work processes, add errors, or make the workspace unsafe.

- **Sort** — Sort through and sort out unneeded items
- **Shine** – Clean and create good cleaning habits
- **Set in Order** –Best location based on usage and workflow
- **Standardize** – Create the rules, visuals and expectations
- **Sustain** – Methods to reinforce the habits and expectations

Organizations practicing **5S** routinely apply the steps above to ensure workspaces are clean, functioning and efficient to ensure employees are able to perform work tasks in the best and most efficient way possible.

Visual workspaces allow employees to:

- **Determine best location for items in the workspace depending on usage**
- **Be able to quickly identify and retrieve items for the workspace**
- **Be able to identify missing or out of place items**
- **Set limits and replenishment rules**

Below list possible areas in your workspace which could be improved by utilizing a 5S program.

_____

_____

_____

_____

_____

_____

_____

_____

Batch Reduction
Identifying optimal batch size to allow continuous work flow

Everything else being equal, a batch of 5 will move through a process faster than a batch of 10. Likewise, a batch of 2 will move faster than a batch of 5 and, ultimately, the fastest flow in a process is 1. Reducing batch size speeds flow. Physically transporting items between process steps not located in the same area can hinder batch reduction.

- **Methods to reduce batch size:**
    - ○ **Organize work steps so work flows easily from one to the next**
    - ○ **Organize work stations so movement of items is simple and continuous**
    - ○ **Minimize the NVA time in a process**
- **Reducing batch size to speed flow**
- **Process orders daily vs. once per week**

When a process is fed by a batch process Workload Balancing issues should be addressed and cross training should be increased for optimal flow.

Could batch reduction be beneficial in your work setting? List possibilities below

_____

_____

_____

_____

_____

_____

_____

_____

_____

Cross-Training

Multiple people trained on each job, and each person trained on multiple jobs. People working together to maximize customer satisfaction and minimize waste.

Cross-Training employees provides more flexibility in the workplace and allows shifts, vacations and illnesses to be covered. Staffing can be adjusted to meet demand. It can also help to reduce boredom and improve job satisfaction. It helps to keep employees challenged and encourages sharing and development of best practices.

Cross-Training helps:
- **Test the process**
- **Expose any problems with the process**
- **Build mutual respect**
- **To better understand the process**
- **Lead to better understanding**

Does your workplace utilize cross-training? List ways it does or possibilities where it could.

_____

_____

_____

_____

_____

_____

_____

_____

_____

_____

_____

Workload Balancing

Optimal work distribution which improves work flow

Building on the concept of continuous, smooth process flow, Workload Balancing enables:

- **Employee allocation**
- **Cross-training**
- **Maximum utilization of people**
- **Making a process more predictable**
- **Workplace equity**

If workloads are not balanced, workers become resentful. When workloads are balanced, the process is more predictable and workers will be happier and more productive. Actions to ensure workload balance may include cross training of workers, especially if the work is cyclical in nature.

Think of ways your work place utilizes or could utilize workload balancing and list them below.

_____

_____

_____

_____

_____

_____

_____

_____

_____

_____

_____

Chapter 6

Creating the Ideal State

As we continue to identify targets for improvement in your process, the next step is to imagine the **Ideal State** of your process without any constraints. What would your process be if there were no barriers or if all the resources needed were readily available?

To Create the Ideal State:
- Brainstorm perfect conditions of the process
- Create a wish list for the new process
- Expand the box
- Be creative, the sky is the limit

The **Ideal State** will not be created as a map, but rather as a list of conditions that describe the best possible scenario and flow of the process.

Take a few moments to jot down your ideas of the Ideal State.

_____

_____

_____

_____

The **Ideal State** helps to identify your long term target condition, what you continue to work toward. Some in Lean may refer to this as your 'True North'.

The next step toward *ideal* is to create an improvement plan that can be achieved within the next six to twelve months. This is referred to as your **Future State**.

On to the Future State

Chapter 7

Mapping the Future State

Now that you better understand what is happening in your current process, including many of its inefficiencies, it's time to decide specifically how you will improve it. As you build your **Future State**:

- Refer to the conditions of your **Ideal State** and reach for what is possible within the next six to twelve months.

- Build an **Action Register** to capture specific tasks for implementing your **Future State**.

- Address color-coded dots (VA/NVA) and provide details on how the steps will change.

- Review *Issues* and *Potential Solutions* to ensure they are addressed in the **Future State Map** or on the **Action Register**.

Creating Your Team's Action Register

♦ **Create action items that are:**

- Specific and detailed

- Use action verbs

Determine	*Document*	*Investigate*
Send	*Collect*	*Provide*
Prepare	*Receive*	*Meet/Discuss*

- Identify the action to be taken and the purpose

- Describe the action so everyone will understand and remember its specifics, even towards the end of the project.

  Incorrect and Vague *action items:*

  WebExtender access
  Excel training

Correct and Specific action items:

> Provide WebExtender access for specialists to view forms online

> Schedule Excel training for frontline staff to track and tabulate students with PACE funding for reporting purposes

♦ Break large tasks into manageable action items.

A common action item is training, yet many steps are involved in providing training. Below is an example of how steps might be broken out so they can be easily accomplished and the team can see progress.

24	Develop a *Tip* sheet of helpful hints for **employees** on webtime entry and e-mail to Kay to handout at training session	2-Sep-08		Karla
25	Develop a *Quick Reference* sheet of helpful hints for **supervisors and time keepers** on webtime entry and e-mail to Kay to handout at training sessions	2-Sep-08		Laura
26	Create outline of training and prepare powerpoint with examples of top 10 errors.	2-Sep-08		Bonnie, Kay
27	Set dates of mandatory 2 hr. training for all payroll approvers at each campus and schedule rooms	14-Aug-08		Kay, Kir
	Create a first draft of e-mails to payroll approvers and employees about upcoming WTE.	31-Jul-08		Bonnie

♦ Identify the roles and responsibilities of the team members.

- **Responsibility (R)** One person on the team to who has responsibility for ensuring action is progressing and provides updates to the team

- **Approver (A)** Use only if needed, the person who must give approval for the action to move forward or be completed. Does not have to be a member of the lean team.

- **Support (S)** People who will help or are needed to complete the action. Can be more than one person and does not have to be part of the lean team.

- **Informed (I)** Sometimes in order to fully implement an action certain people need to be informed or notified for input or buy-in. If needed, this is where you would identify those individuals or groups.

◆ Determine the method to be used to prioritize the Action Items. It can be done by color-coding or numbering according to priority.

Status (Green, Yellow, Red)
Go
On hold
Cancelled
Go
Go
On hold
Complete

Status
1
1
3
5
1
2
Complete

◆ Specify a review and/or target date for each action.

Action Register Example

The action register guides your implementation. It is a working document that will be updated and revised frequently as you work through your implementation tasks. Actions should be worded so that whomever is assigned that action has a clear understanding of their task.

	Action Item	Target date	Review date	R (Responsibility for task)	A (Approval Authority)	S (Support/ resources)	I (Needs to be informed)	Comments	Status (Green, Yellow, Red)
1	Inquire with legal whether citizenship questions can be asked on LOI	Nov. 1	Dec. 1	Vicki, Brenda	Legal		HR Liaisons		Go
2	Pending approval of legal, revise LOI to include citizenship.	Nov. 15	Dec. 1	Brenda	Legal	Deb	HR Liaisons		Go
3	Develop confirmation of hire letter to employee and provide instructions to early access (welcome letter)	Nov. 15	Dec. 1	Vicki, Mike	Carla	Renee, Carol, Diane	HR Liaisons	generation of password	Go
4	Inquire into electronic signature for LOI with Legal	Nov. 1	Dec. 1	Vicki, Brenda	Legal		HR Liaisons		Cancelled
5	Review/improve employee checklist for new employee to start setting up accesses/services	Nov.30	Dec. 1	Carolyn		Lea, Kevin,	Sheryl Rippke, HR Liaisons	Make pretty, coordinate with Sheryl's group	Go
6	Create departmental checklist for new employees	Nov. 30	Dec. 1	Carolyn		Pam, Joan, Soma, Lynette	Sheryl Rippke, HR Liaisons	Create/refine checklist of what systems new employees need & it's sent automatically	Go
7	Change People File	Jan. 15	Dec. 1	Stan, Gloria		Stan, Carol, Bill		Dependency on #7 & #8	Go
8	Add new employee status code to demographic		Dec. 1	Stan, Gloria, Vicki	Vicki	Lea	Group	To support this process	On hold

Essentials for Implementing the New Process

- **Team Members are Accountable:** Each team member takes responsibility for completing activities assigned to them in the *Action Register*. The members of the team hold each other accountable to stay on target to make improvements.

- **Follow-up Meetings:** The team will determine how often they will meet to monitor the progress being made toward implementation of the new process.

> *Research supports teams meeting every two weeks as the ideal time period. It has been found that if the time between meetings is stretched to a month, the members often become lost in their regular daily tasks and lose their enthusiasm and interest in the change effort.*

- **Communication of Decisions Made:** The team will determine how and when to communicate the details of the decisions made as a result of *process mapping*.

  - *Are there affected groups inside the process that need to be informed about the decisions and changes implemented?*

  - *What is the best avenue to give feedback to management on the outcomes?*

Tips for Successful Lean Implementation and Measurement of the New Process...

- ✓ Determine what and how to measure process improvements to show success

- ✓ Monitor these measurements to identify issues and if revisions are needed

- ✓ Remain flexible if roadblocks materialize you may need to plan a phased-in approach

- ✓ Follow a strict plan for follow-up actions and dates

- ✓ Celebrate successes!

- ✓ Revisit within 6 months to assure sustainability and determine next steps for continuous improvement

Time to get to work!

Project Metric Examples

Gourmet Dinner Fundraisers	Spring '11	Today	% Change
Process steps approx.	38	15	61%
Processing time for 16 events (1/2 year)	40 hrs.	8 hrs.	80%
Handoffs	6	4	33%
Elapsed time between donor attending a dinner and donor receiving acknowledgement for that dinner -maximum	6 months	7 days	96%
Error rate (items requiring extra processing due to data discrepancies or errors in processing)	42% (48/ 114)	<3%	93%
Databases used to track dinner information	2	1	50%

Payroll	Year 1	Year 2	% Change
Process steps	78	49	37%
Decisions	21	8	62%
Hand-offs	31	18	42%
Staff Overtime to process payroll	463	223	52%
Paper timesheets processed	2035	280	86%
Timesheet errors	1032	497	52%
Paper leave forms	126	11	91%

Student Scholarship Process	2008	2011	% Change
Application types	6	1	83%
Number of scholarships awarded	334	1049	68%
Total dollars awarded	$252,355	$621,448	60%
Number of processing steps	74	50	32%
Processing time (application close to award notification)	189 days	24 days	87%
Handoffs (arrows)	22	12	46%

Team Member Contract

As a team member of this Lean project I understand my role in implementation of the improved process and take responsibility:

1. for completing or helping to complete action items assigned to me or my committee

2. to identify additional action items needed to help implement this project

3. for sharing any and all concerns I have about the implemented process

4. to question the value of each action

5. for communicating the implementation plan and its progress with my colleagues

6. to support this group and their efforts in achieving the desired future state

Signature: _____

Date: _____

The first follow-up meeting is set for _____

Steps that I need to take prior to the follow-up meeting are:

www.workplacelean.org

Lean Terminology

A3 Report: This "A3" sized (11 inches x 17 inches) form is used at Toyota as a one-sheet problem evaluation, root cause analysis, and corrective action planning tool. It often includes sketches, graphics, flow maps or other visual means of summarizing the current condition and future state.

Andon Board: A visual control device used to show the current status of the process and/or system. The visual control usually takes the form of a lighted overhead display or series of lights that can signal normal and abnormal conditions in the process.

Autonomation: A machine or process that immediately stops whenever a defect or abnormal condition occurs. This technique is an essential element in introducing one-piece flow to a process. Also referred to as Jidoka. Compare to Mistake Proofing.

Balanced Production: When a manufacturing system/entity produces "exactly" (+ or -) what their customers demand.

Batch-and-Queue: A processing method where multiple pieces of work (often referred to as a "batch" or "lot") are processed and/or passed together from one operation to the next. Upon arrival at the next process some or all of these pieces of work may wait in a "queue" to be worked on.

Benchmarking: Comparing key performance metrics with other organization in similar or relevant industries. Establishing standards for improvement based on what others have been able to achieve. Visiting or interviewing peers to learn from what they have done.

Chaku-Chaku: A production line where the only human activity is to 'chaku' or 'load' the machines. The machines eject the finished parts automatically using hanedashi, so that the operators do not have to wait.

Changeover: The activity of converting a process from performing one type of work to another. Changeover time is the elapsed time from when the last good unit of the run just completed is completed until the first good unit of the following run is completed. Changeovers can be physical (changing a fixture) or mental (orienting one's self with the next "job"). Long changeovers often result in batch processing, inhibiting the ability to achieve one-piece-flow.

Continuous Flow Production: A work process management system wherein workers only work on one unit at a time and only one unit of work moves from process to process. Implementation of continuous flow can have significant impact on reducing throughput time, minimizing waste and improving value adding activity. This concept is also referred to as Single Piece Flow or One Piece Flow. Contrast with Batch and Queue.

Cycle Time: The frequency, or interval, of work being completed. Compare to Process Time, contrast with Lead Time.

Error Proofing: See Mistake Proofing

Five S (5S): An approach utilizing workplace organization and visual controls to improve performance. It is derived from the Japanese words seiri, seiton, seiso, seiketsu and shitsuke. The English equivalents are sort, set-in-order, shine, standardize and sustain. Safety is often referred to as the sixth "S," but in traditional 5S programs safety is assumed to be predominant throughout.

Flow: The smooth, uninterrupted movement of a product or service through a series of process steps. In true flow, the work product (information, paperwork, material, etc.) passing through the series of steps never stops.

Functional Layout: The grouping and management of resources based on similar activities or operations, as opposed to physically arranging and managing a work team based on the sequence of process steps. An example would be where all the design engineers sit together, separate from the drafting staff.

Future State Map: A plan for how a process is planned to be running at a defined point in time in the future. Serves as the primary input for the development of an implementation plan. Future State Value Stream Maps are usually developed looking 3 – 12 months into the future. Also referred to as the ideal state, blue sky state or nirvana state.

Heijunka: The leveling of quantities and types of products/services produced for the customer.

Information Flow: The movement of information through a process or organization.

Inventory Turns: The number of times you can "Turn" (use and replace) your inventory/money over in a year

Jidoka: see Autonomation

Just-in-Time (JIT): A production system to make what the customer needs when the customer needs it in the quantity the customer needs, using minimal resources of manpower, material, and machinery. The three elements to making Just-in-Time possible are Takt time, Flow production, and the Pull system.

Kaizen: An improvement philosophy in which continuous incremental improvement occurs over a sustained period of time, creating more value and less waste, resulting in increased speed, lower costs and improved quality. When applied to a business enterprise, it refers to ongoing improvement involving the entire workforce including senior leadership, middle management and frontline workers. Kaizen is also a philosophy that assumes that our way of life (working, social or personal) deserves to be constantly improved.

Kanban: A type of Pull Production System whereby the downstream process signals the upstream process to replenish what has been consumed. Kanbans typically pull by part number. Kanban means signboard in Japanese.

Lead Time: The amount of time it takes for a product (or service) to go through the system, from the first operation to the final operation, including processing, delays, movement, queues, etc. At a process level, the process lead time begins when the work is received, and ends when the work is delivered to the next downstream customer. Lead Time = Process Time plus Wait Time (or delays). Also referred to as Throughput Time or Turnaround Time.

Mistake Proofing: A device or procedure designed to prevent the generation of defects. The English translations for this Japanese phrase are: poka means "error" and yoke is "to avoid." Also referred to as Poka-yoke.

Muda, Mura, Muri: A Japanese word for waste.

PDCA (Plan, Do, Check, Act): The basic steps to be followed in making continuous incremental improvements (kaizen). This is also called the Shewhart cycle, named after Walter Shewhart and popularized by W. Edwards Deming.

Poka-Yoke: See Mistake Proofing.

Process: An operation or group of operations that receives inputs, performs an activity and then provides outputs to an internal or external customer.

Process Time: The amount of time is takes to perform a task (or series of tasks) if one could work on it uninterrupted. For example, if one enters data for two minutes, places a call to obtain additional information and waits for ten minutes for the call to be returned, talks with the information supplier for three minutes and finishes data entering in one minute, the process time is six (6) minutes (2 + 3 + 1). Process Time plus wait time (or delays) = Lead Time. This time is related to Takt Time such that if every operation in a complete process has a Process Time equal to or less than the Takt Time, then the product or service can be made in One-piece Flow.

Pull System: A Work In Process (WIP) management approach whereby the downstream process authorizes upstream production through the consumption of work. Common pull systems include One-piece Flow, Kanban and FIFO Lanes.

Quality Function Deployment (QFD): A methodology involving a cross-functional team to reach consensus about final product specifications based on the wishes of the customer.

Queue Time: The amount of time that product, people, information or material waits to be worked on. Also referred to as "wait time".

Sequential Changeover: Also sequential set-up. In a flow process, when changeover times are within Takt Time, changeovers can be performed one after another. Sequential changeover assures that the lost time for each process in the line is minimized to one 'Takt' beat. A set-up team or expert follows the operator, so that by the time the operator has made one round of the flow line (at Takt time), it has been completely changed over to the next product.

Single Minute Exchange of Dies (SMED): A system of set-up reduction and quick changeover pioneered and developed by Shigeo Shingo.

Single-Piece Flow: See Continuous Flow Production

Standard Work: Documentation of the best known method for completing a task or activity. This becomes the way for everyone working on that process to perform the work. This also becomes the baseline for future work. In the words of Taichii Ohno, "where there is no standard, there can be no kaizen (improvement)."

Takt Time: The pace at which work must be completed to meet customer demand. To calculate, divide the available work time by the customer demand for that period. For example, if a call center receives 900 calls per shift, and there are 27,000 seconds of available work time, the takt time is 30 seconds per call. Therefore, one call must be completed every 30 seconds to meet customer demand. Takt, a German word meaning pace, is the heartbeat of any Lean system. Process Time divided by Takt Time yields the number of workers required to support a specific product.

Total Productive Maintenance (TPM): Aims at maximizing equipment effectiveness and uptime throughout the entire life of the equipment.

Value-Added: Any activity, which, from the ultimate customer's perspective is of value, such that the customer is willing to pay for that activity, or that that activity is a condition of doing business with that customer,

Value-Stream Mapping (VSM): A high-level, visual representation of all of the process steps (both VA and NVA) required to transform a customer requirement into a delivered good or service. A VSM shows the connection between information flow and product flow, as well as the major process blocks and barriers to flow. VSMs are used to document current state conditions as well as design a future state. One of the key objectives of Value Stream Mapping is to identify non-value adding activities for elimination. Value Stream Maps, along with the Value Stream Implementation Plan are strategic tools used to help identify, prioritize and communicate continuous improvement activities.

Work in Progress (WIP): Any work that has been initiated or available to be worked on and yet released to the downstream customer

Lean is about challenging the way things are done and learning to see improvement opportunities. The environment in which an organization operates will continue to change. Lean can help organizations adapt effectively to those changes.

Lean becomes THE way of doing business